Country Threads
Goes to Charm School
19 Little Quilts from 5" Squares

Mary Etherington and Connie Tesene

Martingale®
& COMPANY

Country Threads Goes to Charm School:
19 Little Quilts from 5" Squares
© 2010 by Mary Etherington and Connie Tesene

Martingale®
& COMPANY

That Patchwork Place®

That Patchwork Place® is an imprint of
Martingale & Company®.

Martingale & Company
19021 120th Ave. NE, Suite 102
Bothell, WA 98011-9511 USA
www.martingale-pub.com

Printed in China
15 14 13 12   8 7 6 5 4

**Library of Congress Cataloging-
in-Publication Data is available upon request.**

ISBN: 978-1-60468-006-5

Credits

President & CEO: Tom Wierzbicki
Editor in Chief: Mary V. Green
Managing Editor: Tina Cook
Design Director: Stan Green
Developmental Editor: Karen Costello Soltys
Technical Editor: Robin Strobel
Copy Editor: Marcy Heffernan
Production Manager: Regina Girard
Illustrator: Laurel Strand
Cover & Text Designer: Stan Green
Photographer: Brent Kane

Mission Statement
Dedicated to providing quality products
and service to inspire creativity.

Contents

Welcome to Charm School ≈ 4

THE PROJECTS

Say "Please" ≈ 6

Say "Thank You" ≈ 10

Wash Your Hands Before You Eat ≈ 16

Take Turns ≈ 20

Wipe Your Feet ≈ 24

Use a Napkin ≈ 28

Dress for Success ≈ 32

Walk—Don't Run ≈ 35

Stand Up Straight! ≈ 38

No White Shoes After Labor Day ≈ 42

Don't Interrupt! ≈ 45

Never Take Beer to a Job Interview ≈ 48

Don't Talk with Your Mouth Full ≈ 52

Only Babies Eat with Their Fingers ≈ 55

Break Your Bread, Don't Cut It ≈ 58

Take Compliments Courteously ≈ 62

Don't Break Bread into Your Soup ≈ 65

Eat Slowly, It Took a Long Time to Prepare ≈ 68

Eat Soup with the Side of Your Spoon ≈ 71

Charm School Techniques ≈ 74

About the Authors ≈ 78

Welcome to Charm School

Country Threads' Charm School came about in the fall of 2007 when charm packs, groups of 5" squares within a specific fabric line, became available. Every month we offer a different charm pack and a pattern for a small quilt.

"Stepping out of your comfort zone" initiated the theme of working within a limited number of fabrics and a specific color palette.

The Charm School attendance exploded due to the desire of many quilters to try something new. Another reason we think our customers fall in love with Charm School is that the projects are mostly machine pieced, small, and relatively easy to make. Of course quilters can expand the pattern for a larger project if they choose.

One of our philosophies about quilting is simple, and we tell all of our customers the same thing, "This is not the last quilt you'll ever make." Just sew it and enjoy the process. If you don't like it, give it away—someone else may love it.

When developing these patterns, the fabric sometimes dictated a design. Other times it did not, and we looked at block patterns to get ideas. Inspiration can be found in magazines, nature, carpet designs, home decor, and almost anywhere you look. A Charm School block pattern can be repeated for a bed quilt or combined with another series of blocks, depending on the desired finished project. The charm packs used in the original projects are most likely no longer available, but almost any charm pack can be used.

Some of the titles for these small quilts came from a book of etiquette and others came from staff suggestions during lunchtime conversations. After naming projects for 27 years, we were running low on ideas, so this was a fun way for us to name each quilt in the Charm School collection.

The Charm School club is ongoing at Country Threads for a quarterly fee, and it remains very popular. Finishing kits are available through Country Threads Quilt Shop for a nominal fee, depending on availability of fabric. If you don't have fat quarters, yardage amounts are listed in the fabric requirements for each project. In addition, acrylic templates are available for the templates used in this book. Please support your local quilt shop, or contact Country Threads at 641-923-3893 (www.countrythreads.com).

~ *Mary and Connie*

Say "Please"

This is the quilt that started our Charm School series. Choose charm squares with fabric you really love; then play with the circles and layout, experimenting with different arrangements. If someone wants to borrow your quilt, they have to say "please."

Quilt size: 32½" x 32½"
Finished block: 4½" x 4½"

Materials

Yardages are based on 42"-wide fabric. Fat quarters measure 18" x 20".

25 charm squares, 5" x 5", for center squares
17 charm squares, 4" x 4", for circles (may substitute 5" charm squares)
1 fat quarter *each* of light, medium, and dark fabric for border (3 fat quarters total)
¼ yard of gold tone-on-tone fabric for binding
1 yard of fabric for backing
36" x 36" piece of batting
½ yard of 17"-wide fusible web

Still Charming

If you don't have a set of precut charm squares, you'll need a 5" x 42" strip (or 1 fat quarter) *each* of a minimum of 5 different prints for backgrounds and a 4" x 13" scrap *each* of 6 different prints for circles. (Using additional fabrics will make your quilt look more like the sample.) Cut the background fabrics into a total of 25 squares, 5" x 5". Cut the circles directly from the circle fabrics.

Cutting

Measurements include ¼"-wide seam allowances.

From the fat quarter of light fabric, cut:
3 strips, 5½" x 20"; cut into 20 rectangles, 2¾" x 5½"

From the fat quarter of medium fabric, cut:
3 strips, 5½" x 20"; cut into 20 rectangles, 2¾" x 5½"

From the fat quarter of dark fabric, cut:
4 corner squares, 5½" x 5½"

From the gold tone-on-tone fabric, cut:
4 strips, 1½" x 42"

Assembly

1. Arrange the 5" squares into five rows of five squares each.
2. Using fusible web, the 4" squares, and the patterns on page 9, prepare 5 large circles and 12 small circles for appliqué. (See "Fusible Appliqué" on page 75.) Arrange the circles on the 5" squares until you like how they look. Fuse the circles to the squares.
3. Sew the squares into rows. Press the seam allowances in opposite directions from row to row. Sew the rows together and press.

4. With your sewing machine, zigzag or blanket stitch around each circle.
5. To make the border, sew 10 rectangles together as shown, alternating the light and medium fabrics. Make four borders.

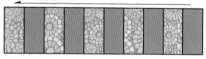

Border.
Make 4.

6. Sew two borders to opposite sides of the quilt top. Press toward the quilt center.
7. Sew a 5½" dark square to each end of the two remaining borders. Sew these borders to the top and bottom of the quilt top.

8. Layer the quilt top with batting and backing; baste. Quilt as desired. Sew the 1½"-wide gold strips together end to end to make one long strip. Use this strip to bind your quilt. (See "Finishing" on page 76.)

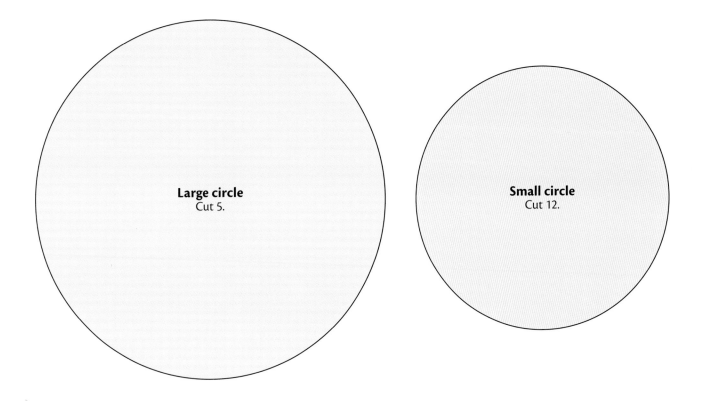

Large circle
Cut 5.

Small circle
Cut 12.

Say "Thank You"

Tumbler-shaped blocks are not often seen, because they require the use of a template. Well, put aside any fears about using templates. They're actually pretty simple, and a small quilt is ideal for trying them out. You'll say "thank you" when you hang this quilt on your wall.

Quilt size: 26" x 18"
Finished block: 3"-tall tumbler

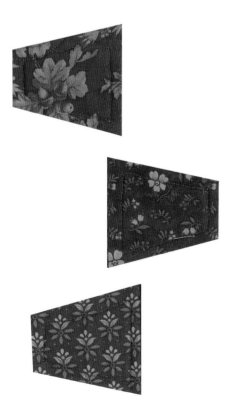

Materials

Yardages are based on 42"-wide fabric.

42 charm squares, 5" x 5", in a range of values for tumblers
⅓ yard of green print for outer border
¼ yard of dark tone-on-tone fabric for letters
¼ yard of dark red print for inner border and binding
⅔ yard of fabric for backing
29" x 21" piece of batting
¼ yard of 17"-wide fusible web
Template plastic★
★*A 3" tumbler acrylic template is also available. Check your local quilt shop or Country Threads.*

Still Charming

If you don't have a set of precut charm squares, you'll need ¼ yard *total* of an assortment of dark brown and red prints and ¼ yard *total* of an assortment of medium to light green, tan, and ivory prints. This is a great project to use those little scraps you couldn't bear to throw away.

Cut as for the charm squares.

Cutting

Measurements include ¼"-wide seam allowances.

Before cutting, separate the charm squares into color families by value. In our case the browns were darkest, followed by the reds and greens, and then the tans and white. If using templates is new to you, see "Working with Templates" on page 75.

From *each* of the charm squares, cut:
1 tumbler using pattern on page 14 (42 total)

From the dark red print, cut:
2 strips, 1" x 42"
3 strips, 1½" x 42"

From the green print, cut:
3 strips, 2½" x 42"

Assembly

1. Arrange the tumblers into six horizontal rows, from darkest to lightest. We made one row brown, two rows red, and one row each of green, tan, and ivory.

2. Sew the tumblers into columns, pressing seam allowances in opposite directions. Sew the columns together. Do not trim the uneven edges at this time.

3. Using the letter patterns on pages 14–15, trace the letters onto fusible web. Remember to trace two of letter "S." Fuse the traced letters onto the dark tone-on-tone fabric, following the manufacturer's instructions. (See "Fusible Appliqué" on page 75.)

4. Position the letters toward the lighter, top part of the quilt and fuse in place.

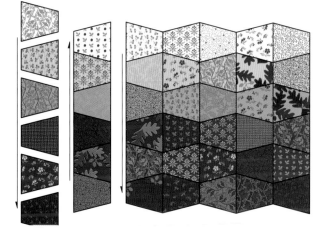

5. Using your sewing machine, zigzag or blanket stitch around letters.

6. Trim the edges of the quilt to square it up. Be careful handling the quilt top, as the edges are now on the bias and will stretch.

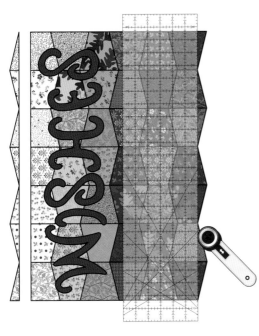

7. Measure the height of the quilt and cut two strips from one of the 1"-wide dark red strips to this length. Sew the strips to the sides of the quilt and press the seam allowances toward the strips. Measure the width of the quilt and trim the remaining 1"-wide red strips to this measurement. Sew these strips to the top and bottom of the quilt top and press the seam allowances toward the strips.

8. Repeat step 7 using the 2½"-wide strips of green print to make the outer border. See illustration bottom center.

9. Layer the quilt top with batting and backing; baste. Quilt as desired. Sew the 1½"-wide dark red strips together end to end to make one long strip. Use this strip to bind your quilt. (See "Finishing" on page 76.)

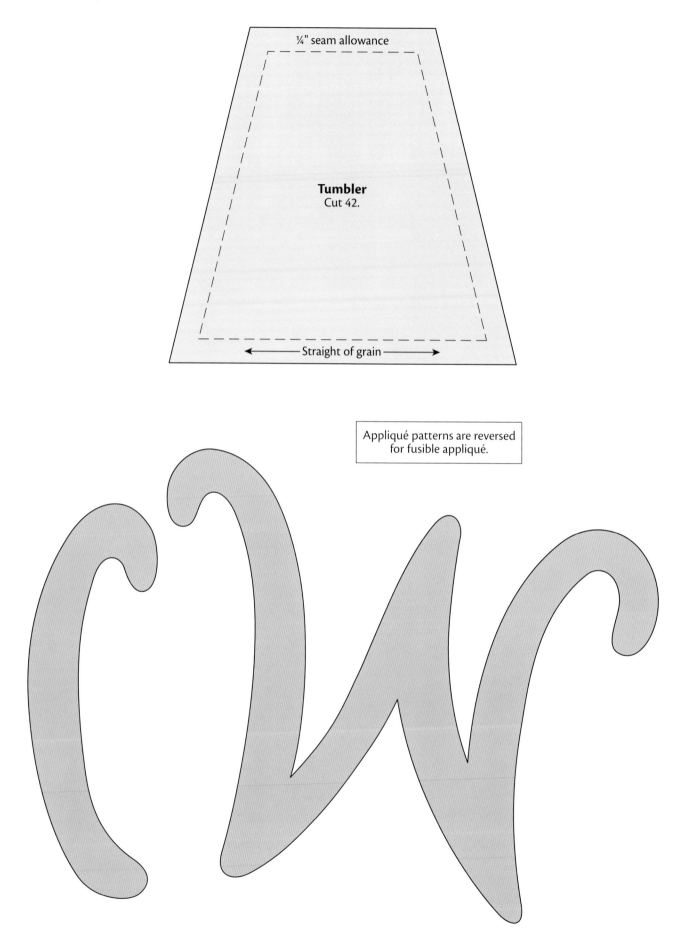

¼" seam allowance

Tumbler
Cut 42.

← Straight of grain →

Appliqué patterns are reversed
for fusible appliqué.

Patterns are reversed
for fusible appliqué.

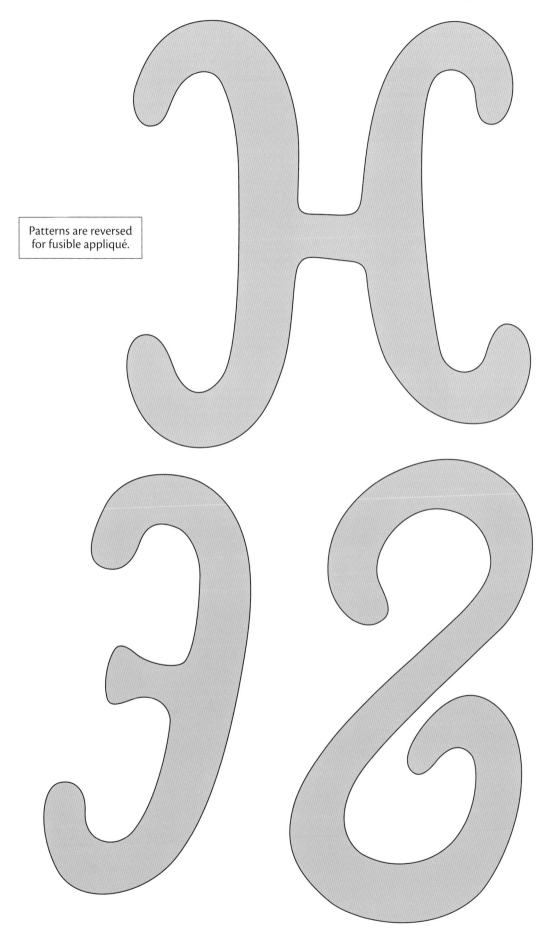

Wash Your Hands Before You Eat

Four Patch blocks with

alternating unpieced squares

is a quiltmaker's classic—just

like parents everywhere

saying, "Wash your hands

before you eat."

Quilt size: 41½" x 49½"

Finished block: 4" x 4"

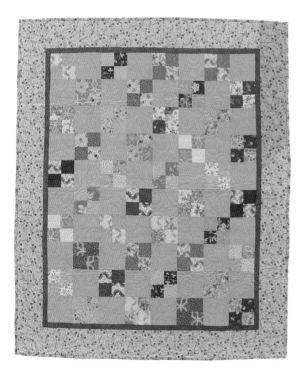

Materials
Yardages are based on 42"-wide fabric.

40 charm squares, 5" x 5", in a range of values for blocks

1 yard of grayish green print for outer border and binding

¾ yard of bluish green striped fabric for alternate squares

¼ yard of red fabric for inner border

2⅝ yards of fabric for backing★

46" x 54" piece of batting

★*See "Country Sense" on page 19.*

Still Charming

If you don't have a set of precut charm squares, you'll need a 5" x 17" strip of at least 14 different prints in a range of values. (Using additional fabrics will make your quilt look more like the sample.) From each print cut 3 squares, 5" x 5" (42 total squares; 2 will be extra). Pair different fabrics in step 1.

Cutting
Measurements include ¼"-wide seam allowances.

From the red fabric, cut:
4 strips, 1¼" x 42"

From the grayish green print, cut:
5 strips, 4½" x 42"
5 strips, 1½" x 42"

Assembly

1. Sort the charm squares into pairs so the fabrics in each pair are noticeably different in value. Make 20 pairs, placing them right sides together.

2. Cut a stacked pair in half vertically and horizontally to yield four sets of squares, 2½" x 2½".

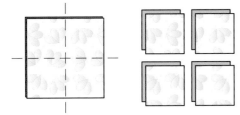

3. Sew each light square to a dark square and press the seam allowances toward the darker fabric. You'll have four identical units from one pair of charm squares (80 total).

Make 4 units
from each pair
of charm squares.

4. Sew two matching units from step 3 together to make a Four Patch block; press. Sew the other two matching units together to make a second Four Patch block; press. Repeat to make a total of 40 Four Patch blocks.

Four-Patch block.
Make 40.

5. Measure your blocks. They should measure about 4½" square. It's OK if they measure a little larger or smaller than that, but if your blocks have much more than ⅛" difference in size between them, trim all your blocks to the smallest size. (See "Squaring Up Blocks" on page 76.)

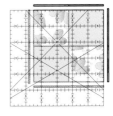

6. From the striped fabric, cut squares the same size as your Four Patch blocks. For example, if your Four Patch blocks measure 4⅜" x 4⅜", cut the squares 4⅜" x 4⅜". Cut 40 striped squares.

7. Alternating the striped squares with the Four Patch blocks, lay out 10 rows with four blocks and four squares per row. Sew the blocks together and press toward the striped squares. Sew the rows together and press.

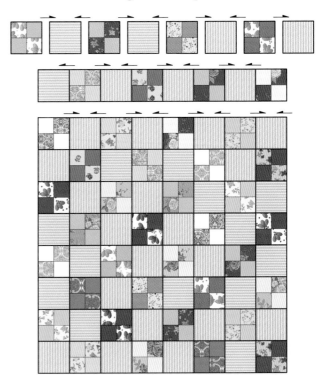

8. Measure the width of the quilt top through the middle and trim two of the red inner-border strips to this measurement. Sew the borders to the top and bottom of the quilt top and press the seam allowances toward the borders.

Measure the length of the quilt top, including the borders just added, and trim the remaining red strips to that length. (If your quilt top is longer than the inner-border strips, sew the remnants from the top and bottom borders to the strips.) Sew the borders to the sides of the quilt top and press toward the borders.

9. Measure the width of the quilt top and trim two of the 4½"-wide grayish green outer-border strips to this measurement. Sew them to the top and bottom of the quilt and press toward the outer border. Join the three remaining 4½"-wide strips end to end and from that long strip, cut two strips to fit the length of the quilt top. Sew the borders to the sides of the quilt and press toward the outer border.

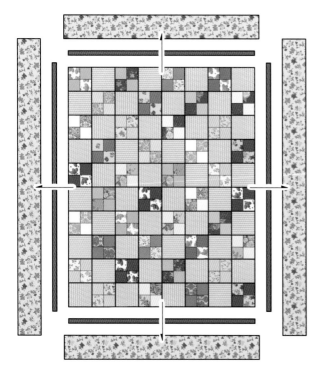

10. Layer the quilt top with batting and backing; baste. Quilt as desired. Sew the 1½"-wide grayish green print strips together end to end to make one long strip. Use this strip to bind your quilt. (See "Finishing" on page 76.)

Country Sense

This quilt is only a little bit wider than the selvage-to-selvage width of most fabric. To save on the amount of backing fabric, buy 1⅝ yards of backing fabric. Then piece a strip, 6½" x 54", using leftover fabrics or scraps from your stash. Cut the 42"-wide backing fabric lengthwise anywhere from 14" to 20" from a selvage edge, and sew the pieced strip between the two pieces of backing. When you baste the quilt layers together, make sure the stripe on the back runs parallel with the seams on the quilt. You have a quilt with a "fancy" back and more money in your pocket.

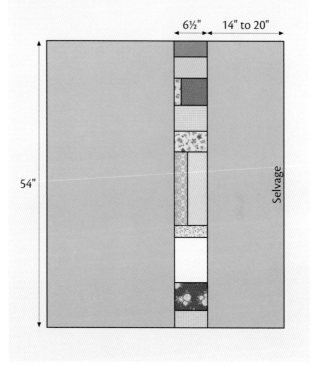

Take Turns

When looking at this quilt, the pinks and browns take turns dominating what you see. Our eyes tend to shift from the star to the diagonal lines of the surrounding blocks. Pink and brown is a classic color combination, but any charm pack with two dominant colors is all you need.

Quilt size: 20" x 30"

Finished block: 4" x 4"

Scrap It Up!

When piecing your leftover scraps for the outer border, don't worry too much about the length of the pieces as long as the border width is the same. You may have to use some of the leftover pink and brown fabric to complete the outer border. Substitute any brown or pink in your fabric collection if you cut incorrectly or need extra fabric. The additional fabrics don't need to match the fabrics within the quilt. Use what you have. It will make your project look even more like a scrappy antique doll quilt.

Materials

Yardages are based on 42"-wide fabric.

14 assorted pink charm squares, 5" x 5", for blocks and outer border

14 assorted brown charm squares, 5" x 5", for blocks and outer border

⅓ yard of tan print for blocks and inner border

⅓ yard of pink print for Star block, sashing cornerstones, and border corners

¼ yard of brown print for Star block, sashing strips, and outer border

¼ yard of a different brown print for binding

¾ yard of fabric for backing

24" x 34" piece of batting

Still Charming

If you don't have a set of precut charm squares, you'll need a 3" x 21" strip *each* of seven pink prints and seven brown prints. Double the number of pieces for each charm square in the cutting instructions.

Cutting

Measurements include ¼"-wide seam allowances.

When cutting your charm squares, be very careful not to waste any fabric. Measure to the outside of pinked edges. Do not straighten the edges; you'll need every square inch of fabric.

From *each* pink charm square, cut:

2 squares, 1½" x 1½" (28 total)

1 square, 2⅞" x 2⅞"; cut each square in half diagonally to make 2 triangles (28 total)

1 rectangle 1¾" x 2½" (14 total; you only need 12)

From *each* brown charm square, cut:

2 squares, 2½" x 2½" (28 total)

1 rectangle, 2½" x 5" (14 total)

continued on following page

From the tan print, cut:

2 strips 1⅞" x 42"; cut into 32 squares, 1⅞" x 1⅞".
 Cut each square in half diagonally to make 2
 triangles (64 total)

4 squares, 1½" x 1½"

3 strips 1½" x 42"; cut 1 of the strips into 2 strips,
 1½" x 14½", trim the other 2 strips to 1½" x 26½"

From the pink print, cut:

4 squares, 1⅞" x 1⅞"; cut each square in half
 diagonally to make 2 triangles (8 total)

8 squares, 1½" x 1½"

4 squares, 2½" x 2½"

From the brown print, cut:

4 squares, 1⅞" x 1⅞"; cut each square in
 half diagonally to make 2 triangles (8 total)

3 strips, 1½" x 42"; cut into 22 strips, 1½" x 4½"

2 rectangles, 2½" x 5"

From the brown print for binding, cut:

3 strips, 1½" x 42"

Assembly

Each 4" Charm block is made from one brown
charm square, one pink charm square, and the
tan print. All four pieces of pink and both pieces
of brown print should match within a block. The
Star block is not made with charm squares, but
with the brown, pink, and tan prints.

1. Place a tan triangle right sides together with
 a pink charm square, aligning the short edges
 of the triangle with two sides of the square,
 and stitch. Press the seam allowances toward
 the triangle. Sew the short edge of another
 tan triangle to a side of the pink square as
 shown. Press toward the triangle. Be careful
 not to stretch the long side of the tan triangles.
 Repeat to make two units from each pink
 charm square fabric (14 matching pairs).

Make 14 pairs.

2. Sew a 2⅞" pink charm triangle to each of the
 units from step 1, matching fabrics. You will
 have 14 matching units (28 total).

Make 14
matching units.

3. Arrange two matching units from step 2 with
 two matching brown squares so the pink
 squares are on the outside of the block. Sew
 the squares and units together and press. Make
 14 Charm blocks.

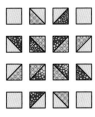

Make 14.

4. For the Star block, sew four pink print 1⅞"
 triangles to four tan triangles as shown. Sew
 four brown print triangles to four tan triangles.
 Sew four pink print triangles to four brown
 print triangles. Press the seam allowances as
 shown.

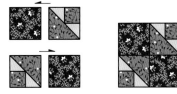

Make 4 of each.

5. Arrange the triangle units from step 4 with
 four tan 1½" squares as shown. Sew into rows
 and sew the rows together. It can be difficult
 to press the seam allowances in a direction that
 makes it easy to match the points. One solution
 is to press the seam allowances open instead of
 to one side.

Make 1.

6. Arrange the 14 Charm blocks and the Star block in three columns of five blocks per column with the Star block in the center. We oriented all of the Charm blocks in the same direction. Place a brown print 1½" x 4½" sashing strip between each block. Alternating five sashing strips and four cornerstones as shown, arrange a sashing row between each block row. Sew into rows and sew the rows together. Press toward the sashing strips.

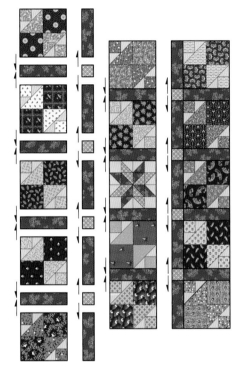

7. For the inner border, sew the tan 1½" x 14½" strips to the top and bottom of the quilt top, easing as needed to fit. Sew the tan 1½" x 26½" strips to the sides of the quilt top. Press toward the borders.

8. The outer border is made from the leftover fabrics. Your brown rectangles should measure about 2½" x 5". The 2½" measurement is the border width. If the scraps are a little narrower, trim them all to the narrowest width (either 2¼", or 2"). Trim the pink 1¾" x 2½" rectangles and the four 2½" squares to this same width. For example, if your border pieces are 2¼", cut the pink rectangles 1¾" x 2¼" and the corner squares 2¼" x 2¼".

9. Sew two pink rectangles between three brown rectangles to make a side border. Make two, and check the fit. Borders are too long? Just trim to fit. Borders are too short? Substitute the brown print for one of the rectangles and cut it longer than the others. Sew the side borders to the quilt top. Press toward the inner border. Sew four pink rectangles between five brown rectangles to make the top border. Check the fit and add or trim as needed. Sew a pink print corner square to each end. Repeat to make the bottom border. Sew the top and bottom borders to the quilt top. Press toward the inner border.

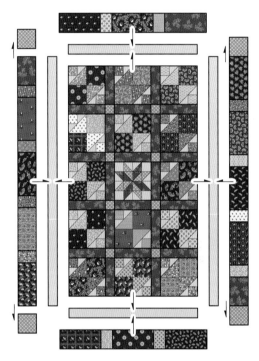

10. Layer the quilt top with batting and backing; baste. Quilt as desired. Sew brown 1½"-wide binding strips together end to end to make one long strip. Use this strip to bind your quilt. (See "Finishing" on page 76.)

Wipe Your Feet

The blocks in this quilt resemble four small trees that meet in the center in a miniature forest. And remember, after tromping through the farm or the woods, wipe your feet before entering the house.

Quilt size: 26" x 26"
Finished block: 6" x 6"

Materials

Yardages are based on 42"-wide fabric.

20 charm squares, 5" x 5", in a mixture of medium to dark values in brown, red, and green for "trees" and cornerstones

½ yard of brown print for sashing, inner border, and binding

⅜ yard of olive green plaid for outer border

⅛ yard of tan print for block backgrounds

⅛ yard of a different tan print for block backgrounds

⅛ yard of dark brown or black print for tree trunks

1 yard of fabric for backing

30" x 30" piece of batting

Still Charming

If you don't have a set of precut charm squares, you'll need a 4" x 8" strip *each* of nine different prints in medium to dark values in brown, red, and green, and a 4" x 4" scrap of light brown print. (Using additional fabrics will make your quilt look more like the sample.) Cut the light brown print into four squares, 1½" x 1½", for cornerstones. Cut each of the nine different prints into two squares, 3⅞" x 3⅞" (18 total). Cut each of these squares in half diagonally to make two triangles (36 total).

Cutting

Measurements include ¼"-wide seam allowances.

From *each* of 2 of the lightest value charm squares, cut:
2 squares, 1½" x 1½" (4 total)

From *each* of the remaining 18 charm squares, cut:
1 square, 3⅞" x 3⅞"; cut each square in half diagonally to make 2 triangles (36 total)

From the dark brown or black print, cut:
3 strips, 1¼" x 42"

From *each* of the tan prints, cut:
9 squares, 3⅞" x 3⅞" (18 total)

continued on following page

From the brown print, cut:
2 strips, 1½" x 42"; cut into 12 strips, 1½" x 6½"
2 strips, 1½" x 20½"
2 strips, 1½" x 22½"
3 strips, 1½" x 42"

From the olive green plaid, cut:
2 strips, 2½" x 22½"
2 strips, 2½" x 26½"

Assembly

The blocks in this quilt resemble four small trees that meet in the center. Trees opposite one another are made from matching fabric. We used the two different background fabrics in each block throughout the quilt.

1. Press under ¼" on both long edges of the dark brown or black print strips. With right sides facing up, lay each strip diagonally on the 3⅞" tan squares to make tree trunks.

2. Topstitch the tree-trunk strips to the tan squares, stitching close to each long edge. Cut the squares apart.

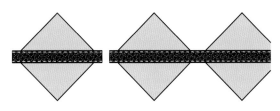

3. Cut each tan square in half diagonally as shown to yield 18 triangles from each of the tan prints (36 total). Trim the tree trunks to the edge of the triangles, keeping triangles of the same fabric together.

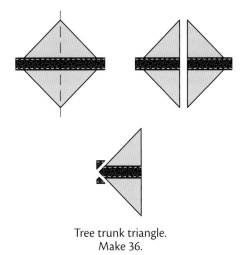

Tree trunk triangle.
Make 36.

4. Sew matching tree-trunk triangles to the charm-square triangles along the long edges. Make two matching tree units.

Tree unit.
Make 18 pairs.

5. Using two matching tree units with one tan print and two matching tree units with the other tan print, sew the pieced units together as you would a Four Patch block. Try and choose two charm square prints that look different from each other. Press seam allowances open. Make a total of nine blocks.

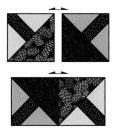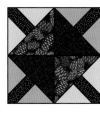

Tree block.
Make 9.

6. Lay out the blocks and 1½" x 6½" brown sashing strips as shown. Position the four 1½" cornerstones. Sew the blocks, sashing, and cornerstones into rows, and then sew the rows together. Press toward the sashing.

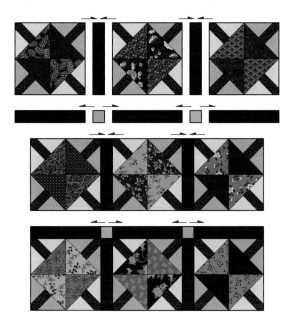

7. For the inner border, sew the 1½" x 20½" brown strips to the sides of the quilt. Press the seam allowances toward the strips. Sew the 1½" x 22½" brown strips to the top and the bottom of the quilt. Press the seam allowances toward the strips. Repeat, using the olive green plaid strips for the outer border.

8. Layer the quilt top with batting and backing; baste. Quilt as desired. Sew the 1½" x 42" brown strips together end to end to make one long strip. Use this strip to bind your quilt. (See "Finishing" on page 76.)

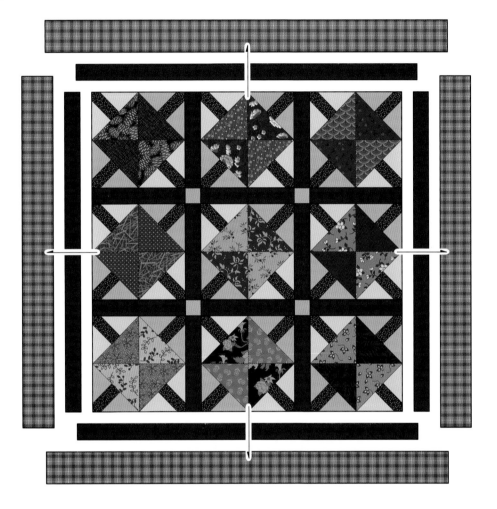

Use a Napkin

Use a charm pack of children's prints or other bright and cheerful fabric for this quilt. And remind the kids, "Don't wipe your fingers on the quilts—use a napkin."

Quilt size: 26" x 30"
Finished block: 4" x 4"

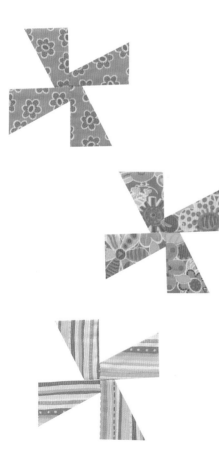

Materials

Yardages are based on 42"-wide fabric.

30 medium- to light-value pastel charm squares, 5" x 5", for blocks
½ yard of white fabric for block background
½ yard of blue-and-white striped fabric for border
¼ yard of pink print for binding
1 yard of fabric for backing
30" x 34" piece of batting
2½" square of template plastic
★*A mini windmill acrylic template for 4" scraps is also available. Check your local quilt shop or Country Threads.*

Still Charming

If you don't have a set of precut charm squares, you'll need one strip each, 2½" x 20", of 10 different pastel prints in medium to light values. (Using additional fabrics will make your quilt look more like the sample.) Cut each strip with the windmill blade template as in step 3 on page 31. Cut 12 blades and make three blocks from each fabric.

Cutting

Measurements include ¼"-wide seam allowances.

From *each* charm square, cut:
2 rectangles, 2½" x 5" (60 total)

From the white fabric, cut:
5 strips, 2½" x 42"

From the blue-and-white striped fabric, cut:
2 strips, 3½" x 30½"
2 strips, 3½" x 20½"

From the pink print, cut:
3 strips, 1½" x 42"

Assembly

1. Make a plastic template of the Windmill Blade pattern on page 31. (See "Working with Templates" on page 75.)

2. Layer two to four 2½" x 5" charm-fabric rectangles *right sides up*, being careful to align all the edges. Use the template to mark two windmill blades on the top fabric. Then use your rotary cutter and ruler to cut on the marked lines through all the layers. Cut all charm-fabric rectangles in the same manner; you'll have four windmill blades from each fabric (120 total).

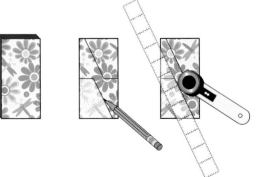

3. If your white fabric has a discernable right and wrong side, cut the 2½"-wide strips in half along the fold line and lay them on top of each other, all with right sides facing up and the edges carefully aligned. (If both sides are identical you can leave the fabric strips folded.) Trace the windmill blade template across the top strip as shown and cut 120 white windmill blades.

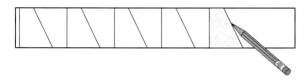

4. Join each charm-fabric windmill blade with the white windmill blades. The pieces align at the ¼" seam and along the diagonal side. Press the seam allowances toward the charm fabric. Make 120 windmill-blade units (30 sets of four with the same fabric).

Make 30 sets
of 4 each (120 total).

5. Join four units with the same fabric as shown. Press the long seam allowances open to reduce bulk. Repeat to make 30 blocks.

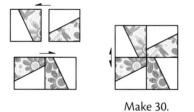

Make 30.

6. Lay out the blocks in six rows of five blocks each. Sew the blocks into rows, and then sew the rows together. Press in the opposite direction from row to row.

7. Sew the 3½" x 20½" striped strips to the quilt top and bottom. Press the seam allowances toward the borders. Sew the 3½" x 30½" striped strips to the sides of the quilt. Press the seam allowances toward the borders.

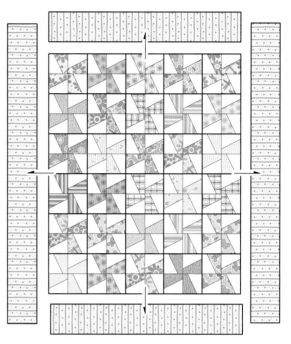

8. Layer the quilt top with batting and backing; baste. Quilt as desired Sew 1½"-wide pink strips together end to end to make one long strip. Use this strip to bind your quilt. (See "Finishing" on page 76.)

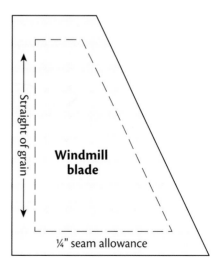

Straight of grain

Windmill
blade

¼" seam allowance

Dress for Success

There are several ways to make triangle squares, also known as half-square-triangle units. The method we employ in this quilt makes the most of the 5" charm squares. There's more than one route to success!

Quilt size: 29" x 29"
Finished block: 4" x 4"

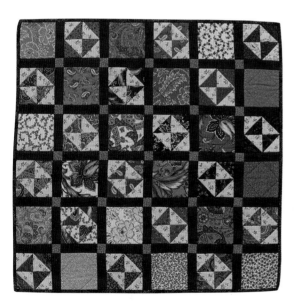

Materials

Yardages are based on 42"-wide fabric.

38 charm squares, 5" x 5", medium-light to dark in value
⅓ yard of light print for block background
⅓ yard of dark brown print for sashing
⅛ yard of salmon print for cornerstones
¼ yard of brown print for binding
1 yard of fabric for backing
33" x 33" piece of batting

Still Charming

If you don't have a set of precut charm squares, you'll need a 5" x 10" piece *each of* at least nine dark-value prints, nine medium-value prints and one light-value print. Cut each of the nine dark prints into two squares, 5" x 5". Cut each of the medium prints into two squares, 4½" x 4½", and cut the light print into two squares, 5" x 5".

Cutting

Measurements include ¼"-wide seam allowances.

Select the two lightest-value charm squares to be used as background squares in two of the blocks. Separate the remaining 36 squares into two stacks: 18 medium- and 18 dark-value squares.

From *each* of the 18 medium-value charm squares, cut:
1 square, 4½" x 4½" (18 total)

From the light print, cut:
2 strips, 5" x 42"; cut into 16 squares, 5" x 5"

From the dark brown print, cut:
7 strips, 1½" x 42"; cut into 60 strips, 1½" x 4½"

From the salmon print, cut:
1 strip, 1½" x 42"; cut into 25 squares, 1½" x 1½"

From the brown print, cut:
3 strips, 1½" x 42"★

★*If you don't have a 42" width of usable fabric, you may need 4 strips.*

Triangle Thangle

We originally wrote this pattern so you could use Thangles to create the triangle squares in step 3. Thangles are sheets of preprinted tear-away paper that make it easy to sew perfect triangle squares. No trimming, no drawing, no measuring—just pin and sew; then cut on the lines and remove the paper. If you'd like to use Thangles, cut the light/dark pairs of 5" squares from step 1 in half to measure 2½" x 5". Pin one pair of 2" Thangles (2" is the finished size of the triangle square) on each half. Sew along the dotted lines and cut on the solid lines. Press; then tear off the paper. Bingo! Four perfect triangle squares. Go to thangles.com for a great video about using Thangles. Check for them at your local quilt shop or Country Threads.

Assembly

1. Pair each of the 18 dark charm squares right sides together with a light background 5" square. (Remember, two of the background squares will be from your charm pack and a little different than your other background squares.)

2. Cut each dark/light pair into quarters that measure 2½" x 2½". Keep squares of the same fabrics together.

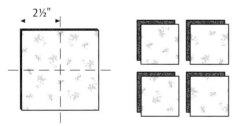

3. With the light fabric on top, mark a diagonal line from corner to corner on the paired 2½" squares. Stitch along the line. Trim so there's a ¼" seam allowance. Press seam allowances toward the dark fabric. Make four matching triangle squares.

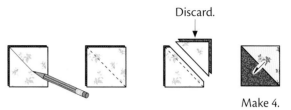

Discard.

Make 4.

4. Combine the four matching triangle squares into a block as shown; press.

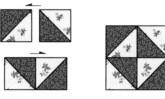

Make 18.

5. Repeat steps 3 and 4 to complete 18 blocks.

6. Arrange the blocks, alternating with the medium-value 4½" squares, in six rows of six blocks each. Place a 1½" x 4½" sashing strip between each to make a block row. Alternate six 4½" sashing strips with 1½" cornerstones as shown to make a sashing row. Sew into rows, and then sew the rows together. Press as shown.

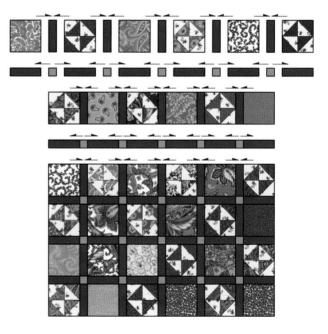

7. Layer the quilt top with batting and backing; baste. Quilt as desired. Sew 1½"-wide brown strips together end to end to make one long strip. Use this strip to bind your quilt. (See "Finishing" on page 76.)

Walk—Don't Run

"Walk—don't run" is usually good advice, unless of course it's Shop Hop time or your favorite quilt store is having a sale.

Quilt size: 23¾" x 38"
Finished block: 4¾" x 4¾"

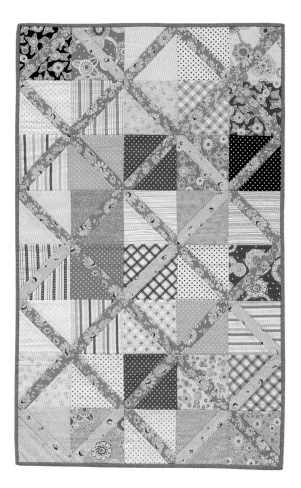

Materials
Yardages are based on 42"-wide fabric.

40 assorted charm squares, 5" x 5", for block background
⅛ yard *each* of 4 coordinating fabrics for blocks
¼ yard of red striped fabric for binding
1⅓ yard of fabric for backing
28" x 42" piece of batting

Still Charming

If you don't have a set of precut charm squares, you'll need a 5" x 10" piece of 20 different fabrics. Cut two squares, 5" x 5", from each fabric for a total of 40 squares. Are 20 different fabrics too many for your stash to supply? You can cut four squares each from a 5" x 20" strip of 10 different prints instead.

Cutting
Measurements include ¼"-wide seam allowances.

From the charm squares, cut:
80 triangles (cut each square in half diagonally)

From *each* of the 4 coordinating fabrics, cut:
2 strips, 1½" x 42"; cut into 10 rectangles, 1½" x 8" (40 total)

From the red striped fabric, cut:
4 strips, 1½" x 42"

Assembly

1. Sew a 1½" x 8" strip between two matching triangles as shown. Press the seam allowances toward the triangles.

2. Trim the excess from the strip and square up the blocks so they measure 5¼" x 5¼".

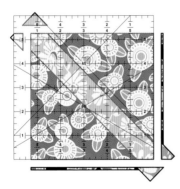

Keeping In Line

It's easy for the triangles to "travel" along the 1½"-wide strip, making your blocks a rectangular shape instead of square. To keep your blocks relatively square, mark the wrong side of the 1½" x 8" rectangles ½" from a short end. Use this mark to align the corners of the triangle.

3. Arrange the blocks in eight rows of five blocks each as shown. Sew the blocks into rows and press seam allowances in opposite directions from row to row. Sew the rows together and press.

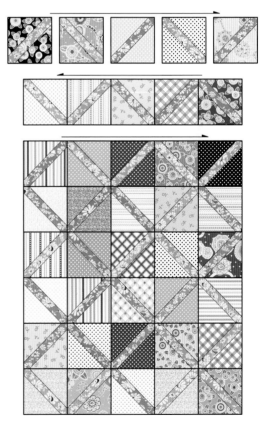

4. Layer the quilt top with batting and backing; baste. Quilt as desired. Sew the 1½"-wide red striped strips together end to end to make one long strip. Use this strip to bind your quilt. (See "Finishing" on page 76.)

Stand Up Straight!

This quilt is simply bursting with energy! We love the flash of turquoise against the hot orange and yellow, but this block looks terrific in all sorts of colors. Give yourself a little push and make this quilt in colors you usually avoid. You'll be "standing tall" when you do.

Quilt size: 15" x 24"
Finished block: 3" x 3"

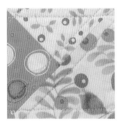

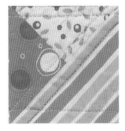

Materials

Yardages are based on 42"-wide fabric.

10 light-, 10 dark-, and 20 medium-value charm squares, 5" x 5", for blocks
⅝ yard of fabric for backing
17" x 26" piece of batting

Still Charming

If you don't have a set of precut charm squares, you'll need 4" x 16" scraps of five different medium-value prints, 4½" x 9" scraps of five different light-value prints, and 4½" x 9" scraps of five different dark-value prints. Cut each medium-value print into four squares, 3⅞" x 3⅞" (20 squares total); then cut each square in half diagonally to yield 40 triangles total. Cut each light-value print into two squares, 4¼" x 4¼"; then cut each square into quarters diagonally to yield four triangles (40 total). Cut each dark-value print as the light-value prints to make 40 dark triangles.

Cutting

Measurements include ¼"-wide seam allowances.

From *each* of the 10 light-value charm squares, cut:
1 square, 4¼" x 4¼"; cut *each* square into quarters diagonally to make 4 triangles (40 total)

From *each* of the 10 dark-value charm squares, cut:
1 square, 4¼" x 4¼"; cut *each* square into quarters diagonally to make 4 triangles (40 total)

From *each* of the 20 medium-value charm squares, cut:
1 square, 3⅞" x 3⅞"; cut *each* square in half diagonally to make 2 triangles (40 total)

From the fabric for backing, cut:
1 piece, 17" x 26"

2. Sew a medium-value triangle to each triangle unit from step 1, stitching along the *long* edge. Press the seam allowances toward the medium-value triangles. Blocks should measure 3½" square. Make 40.

Make 40.

3. Lay out the blocks in eight rows of five blocks each, as shown, with the medium-value triangles in the bottom-right corner.

4. Sew the blocks into rows, pressing in opposite direction from row to row. Sew the rows together and press.

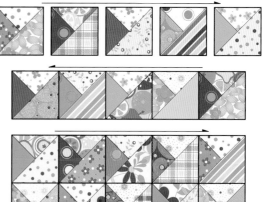

Assembly

1. Sew the dark- and light-value triangles together in pairs, stitching along the *short* edge, with the dark triangle on the left and the light triangle on the right as shown. Mix the fabrics so the combination in each triangle unit is different. Press the seam allowances toward the dark fabric. Make 40 triangle units.

Make 40.

Finishing

This quilt doesn't have binding. Instead, the layers are stitched together and then turned right side out before quilting.

1. Layer the batting, followed by the backing fabric *right side up,* and then the quilt top *right side down.* The batting and backing are a little larger than the quilt. Pin the layers together around the perimeter of the quilt top.

2. Stitch around the edge of the quilt using a ¼" seam allowance and leaving a 6" opening for turning the quilt right side out.

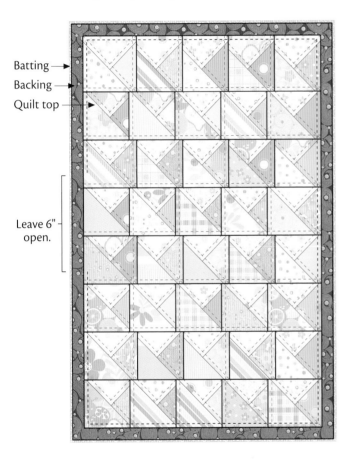

3. Trim the batting and backing to the size of the quilt top, and clip the excess batting out of the corners to reduce bulk.

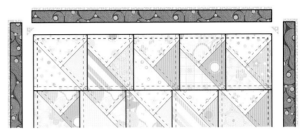

4. Turn the quilt right side out and stitch the opening closed by hand.

5. Press the quilt, and then quilt as desired.

No White Shoes After Labor Day

It doesn't matter what time of year it is—this quilt is pretty enough to hang all year 'round.

Quilt size: 25" x 25"
Finished block: 6" x 6"

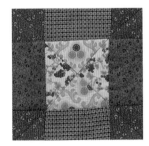

Materials

Yardages are based on 42"-wide fabric.

36 assorted charm squares, 5" x 5", for blocks

½ yard of grayish teal striped fabric for sashing and border

¼ yard of black checked fabric for cornerstones and binding

⅞ yard of fabric for backing

29" x 29" piece of batting

Still Charming

If you don't have a set of precut charm squares, you'll need a 5" x 9" scrap of at least 18 different prints in a range of values. From each print, cut two rectangles, 2" x 3½" (36 total). From nine of the prints, cut one square each, 4¼" x 4¼". Cut these squares into quarters diagonally to yield 36 total triangles. From each of the remaining nine prints, cut four squares, 2" x 2" (36 total).

Cutting

Measurements include ¼"-wide seam allowances.

From 9 of the charm squares, cut:
1 square *each*, 4¼" x 4¼"; cut each square into quarters diagonally to make 4 triangles (36 total)

From 9 of the charm squares, cut:
4 squares *each*, 2" x 2" (36 total)

From 18 of the charm squares, cut:
2 rectangles *each*, 2" x 3½" (36 total)

From the grayish teal striped fabric, cut:
2 strips, 2" x 42"; cut each strip into 6 strips, 2" x 6½" (12 total)
2 strips, 2½" x 21½"
2 strips, 2½" x 25½"

From the black checked fabric, cut:
4 squares, 2" x 2"
3 strips, 1½" x 42"

Assembly

1. Sort the triangles into matching pairs. For each block, you'll need two different pairs of triangles that contrast well with each other. Sew the triangles for each block together to make hourglass units as shown.

Make 9.

2. Select two matching 2" x 3½" rectangles and sew them to opposite sides of an hourglass unit from step 1. Press the seam allowances toward the rectangles. Make 9.

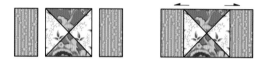

3. Select another pair of matching rectangles for the block, along with a set of four 2" squares. The squares should all match one another, but contrast with the rectangles. Sew a square to each end of each rectangle. Press the seam allowances toward the rectangles. Sew to the top and bottom of a unit from step 2. Repeat for all nine blocks.

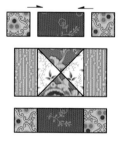 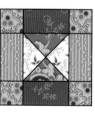

Make 9.

4. Lay out the blocks in three rows of three blocks each. Place 2" x 6½" grayish teal sashing strips between the blocks to make a block row. Alternate three grayish teal sashing strips with two black 2" squares as shown to make a sashing row. Sew into rows, and then sew the rows together. Press toward the sashing strips.

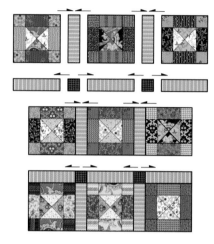

5. Add the 21½"-long grayish teal strips to sides of the quilt. Press the seam allowances toward the grayish teal strips. Sew the 25½"-long grayish teal strips to the top and bottom of the quilt in the same manner.

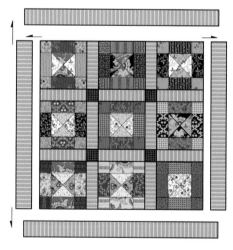

6. Layer the quilt top with batting and backing; baste. Quilt as desired. Sew the 1½"-wide black checked strips together end to end to make one long strip. Use this strip to bind your quilt. (See "Finishing" on page 76.)

Don't Interrupt!

A perfect gift for the hectic

holidays, this quilt won't take

too much time and is simple

to make. You might even

get it made without being

interrupted!

Quilt size: 24" x 24"
Finished block: 4" x 4"

Materials

33 Christmas print charm squares, 5" x 5",
    for blocks
¼ yard of brown Christmas print for border
¼ yard of dark red print for binding and blocks
1 yard of fabric for backing
28" x 28" piece of batting

Still Charming

If you don't have a set of precut charm
squares, you'll need a 1½" x 42" strip of at
least 15 different Christmas prints, 4 of them
predominantly red. From each strip cut seven
rectangles, 1½" x 4½" (105 total, 5 will be
extra). You do not have to cut the 1½" x 4½"
rectangle from the dark red binding fabric.

Cutting

From *each* of the charm squares, cut:
3 rectangles, 1½" x 4½" (99 total; see illustration
    below)

From the brown Christmas print, cut:
2 strips, 2½" x 20½"
2 strips, 2½" x 24½"

From the dark red print, cut:
3 strips, 1½" x 42"; from 1 of these strips,
    cut 1 rectangle, 1½" x 4½"

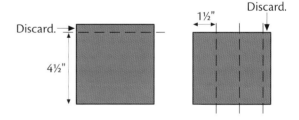

Careful Color Placement

Take care to position the red (or your most dominant color) strips on the outside edge of most of your blocks so that when they're set together, you can form the rail fence pattern that runs through the quilt top. If you're using the "Still Charming" option, you'll have three red and two other rectangles left over.

Assembly

1. Sew the 1½" x 4½" rectangles together in pairs. (One rectangle comes from the red binding fabric.) Sew two pairs together to make a four-rectangle block. Repeat to make 25 blocks total.

Make 25.

2. Lay out the blocks in five rows of five blocks each, alternating the direction of the rails from horizontal to vertical. Study the diagrams when placing the red strips. If you choose to discard a red strip that isn't as dark as the others, you can use leftover dark red binding fabric for the red rails.

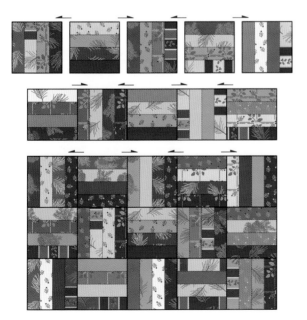

3. When you're satisfied with the block arrangement, sew the blocks into rows, and then sew the rows together. Press.

4. Sew the 20½"-long brown border strips to the top and bottom of the quilt top and press the seam allowances toward the borders. Repeat, using the 24½"-long brown strips for the sides of the quilt.

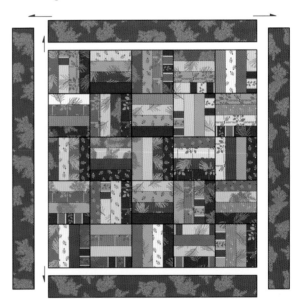

5. Layer the quilt top with batting and backing; baste. Quilt as desired. Sew the 1½"-wide dark red strips together end to end to make one long strip. Use this strip to bind your quilt. (See "Finishing" on page 76.)

Never Take Beer to a Job Interview

There are many rules for polite behavior, but in Country Threads Charm School there is only one hard-and-fast rule, known as the "3 C's rule." Cut Charms Carefully. Oh yes. And don't take beer to a job interview.

Quilt size: 14" x 16"
Finished block: 3" x 3"

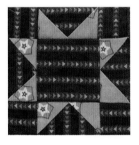

Materials

Yardages are based on 42"-wide fabric.

40 assorted 5" charm squares, 5" x 5", in a range of values for blocks and borders
¼ yard of brown print for binding
⅝ yard of fabric for backing
18" x 20" piece of batting

Still Charming

If you don't have a set of precut charm squares, you'll need a 3" x 42" strip of at least 16 different prints in a range of values. (Using additional fabrics will make your quilt look more like the sample.) Cut two squares, 5" x 5", from *each* of the 16 fabrics. Place one square in stack 1 and a matching square in stack 2; cut into all of the pieces as instructed for both stack 1 *and* stack 2. In addition, cut eight of the strips as for the stack 3 pieces. Keep the pieces from each stack separate. Make two blocks from the same two fabrics, switching the star point and background fabric in each block.

Cutting

Each Star block is made using two fabrics. Presort your charm squares into two piles of 16 squares each. Stack 1 will be used for backgrounds; stack 2 will be used for star points and border squares. The remaining eight charm squares (stack 3) will be used for the border squares. In our quilt, we divided the fabrics so that eight blocks had light/medium points and dark backgrounds and the other eight blocks had darker points and light/medium backgrounds.

Refer to the diagram on page 50 for guidance in cutting. Remember to cut charms carefully!

continued on following page

From *each* of the 16 charm squares in stack 1, cut:

1 square, 2¾" x 2¾"; cut each square into quarters diagonally to make 4 quarter-square triangles (64 total)

1 square, 2" x 2" (16 total)

4 squares, 1¼" x 1¼" (64 total)

From *each* of the 16 charm squares in stack 2, cut:

4 squares, 1⅝" x 1⅝"; cut each square in half diagonally to make 8 triangles (128 total)

2 squares, 1½" x 1½" (32 total)

From *each* of the 8 charm squares in stack 3, cut:

6 squares, 1½" x 1½" (48 total)

From the brown print, cut:

2 strips, 1½" x 42"

Stack 1.
Background.

Stack 2.
Star points
and border.

Stack 3.
Border.

Assembly

Instructions are given for one block. Remember, each block is made using two fabrics. Make 16 blocks.

1. Sew a 1⅝" star-point triangle from stack 2 to either side of a 2¾" triangle from stack 1. Press seam allowances toward the star points. Make four.

Make 4 for each block.

2. Arrange the units from step 1 with a 2" x 2" square, and four 1¼" squares of the same background fabric. Sew together in rows; then sew the rows together. Press as indicated.

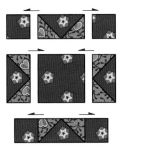 

Make 16.

3. Lay out the Star blocks in four rows of four blocks each. Sew the blocks into rows and press rows in opposite directions. Sew the rows together and press.

4. For the top and bottom border, randomly select 12 of the 1½" squares from stack 2 and stack 3 and sew them together in a row to make a border. Press the seam allowances all in one direction. Make two. Sew the borders to the top and bottom of the quilt and press.

5. For the side borders, sew the remaining 1½" squares together to make 14 four-patch units. Sew seven units together for each border. Join the borders to the sides of the quilt. Press.

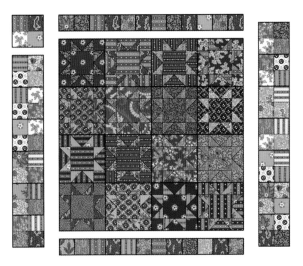

6. Layer the quilt top with batting and backing; baste. Quilt as desired. Sew the 1½"-wide brown strips together end to end to make one long strip. Use this strip to bind your quilt. (See "Finishing" on page 76.)

Don't Talk with Your Mouth Full

We think of this as a "happy quilt," because the interplay of light and dark squares makes us smile. That's *not* what happens when you talk with your mouth full!

Quilt size: 21" x 21"
Finished block: 3½" x 3½"

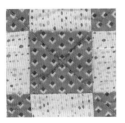

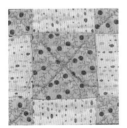

Materials
Yardages are based on 42"-wide fabric.

36 assorted charm squares, 5" x 5", for blocks
½ yard of light print for block background
¼ yard of brown print for binding
¾ yard of fabric for backing
25" x 25" piece of batting

Still Charming

If you don't have a set of precut charm squares, you'll need a 2½" x 20" strip of at least 12 different prints. (Using additional fabrics will make your quilt look more like the sample.) Triple the cutting instructions to make three blocks from the same fabric.

Cutting
Measurements include ¼"-wide seam allowances.

From *each* of the charm squares, cut:
1 square, 2½" x 2½" (36 total)
4 squares, 1¼" x 1¼" (144 total)

From the light print, cut:
9 strips, 1¼" x 42"; cut into 144 rectangles,
    1¼" x 2½"

From the brown print, cut:
3 strips, 1½" x 42"

Assembly
Each block is made with one charm square fabric and four light print rectangles. Piecing instructions are for one block. Make 36 blocks.

1. Sew a 1¼" square to each end of a 1¼" x 2½" rectangle. Press the seam allowances toward the squares. Make 2.

Make 2.

2. Sew a 1¼" x 2½" rectangle to each side of a 2½" square. Press toward the square.

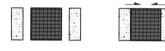

Make 1.

3. Sew the units from step 1 and step 2 together as shown. Press.

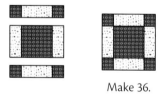

Make 36.

4. Arrange the blocks in six rows of six blocks each. When you're pleased with the arrangement, sew the blocks into rows. Press all seam allowances in opposite directions from row to row; then sew the rows together. Press.

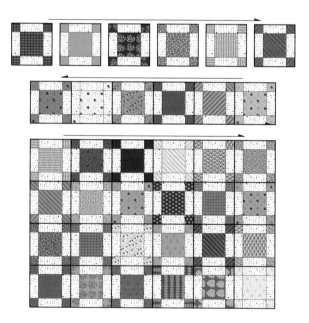

5. Layer the quilt top with batting and backing; baste. Quilt as desired. Sew 1½"-wide brown print strips together end to end to make one long strip. Use this strip to bind your quilt. (See "Finishing" on page 76.)

Only Babies Eat with Their Fingers

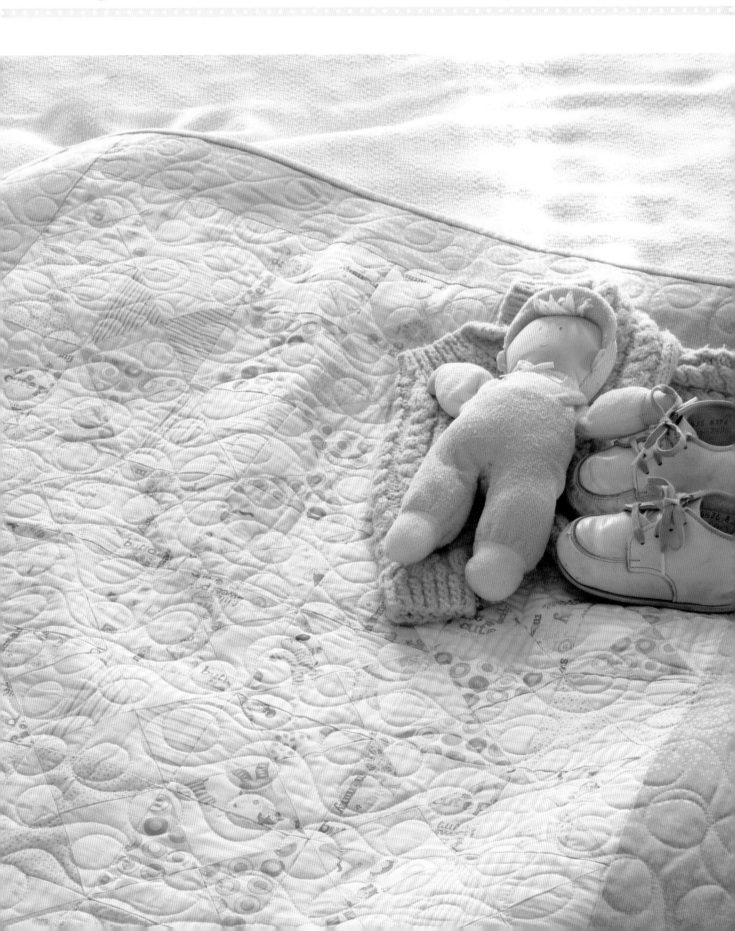

Everybody needs a baby quilt at one time or another. Whip one up for a quick shower gift, or for a special little one.

Quilt size: 32¼" x 36"
Finished block: 3¾" x 3¾"

Materials

Yardages are based on 42"-wide fabric.

28 charm squares, 5" x 5", for blocks
⅝ yard of yellow striped fabric for blocks
⅔ yard of green print for border and binding
1⅛ yard of fabric for backing
36" x 40" piece of batting

Still Charming

If you don't have a set of precut charm squares, you'll need a 5" x 10" strip of 14 different fabrics. (Using additional fabrics will make your quilt look more like the sample.) Cut each strip into two squares, 5" x 5". You'll have four identical blocks per fabric.

Cutting

Measurements include ¼"-wide seam allowances.

From the yellow striped fabric, cut:
4 strips, 5" x 42"; cut into 28 squares, 5" x 5"

From the green print, cut:
4 strips, 3½" x 42"
4 strips, 1½" x 42"

Assembly

1. Layer a yellow striped square with a charm square, right sides together. Cut the squares into quarters diagonally.

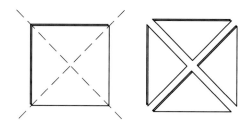

2. With the yellow striped fabric on top of the charm fabric, sew the quarter-square triangles from step 1 together as shown. Start stitching at the right-angle corner and stitch toward the 45° corner. This will create two units with the stripes running vertically and two units with the stripes running horizontally. Press the seam allowances toward the charm fabric.

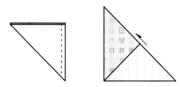

3. Sew a triangle unit with vertical stripes to a triangle unit with horizontal stripes. Repeat to make two blocks. Press the seam allowances in either direction. You'll have two identical blocks per charm fabric. Make a total of 56 Hourglass blocks.

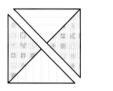

Make 2 blocks
from each charm square
(56 total).

4. Arrange the blocks in eight rows of seven blocks per row as shown. Sew the blocks into rows and press as indicated. Sew the rows together and press.

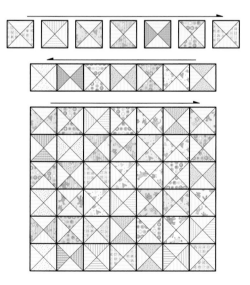

5. Measure the width of the quilt and cut two of the 3½"-wide green strips to this measurement. Sew the borders to the top and the bottom of the quilt. Measure the length of the quilt and cut the remaining two 3½"-wide green strips to this measurement. Sew the borders to the sides of the quilt. Press the seam allowances toward the borders.

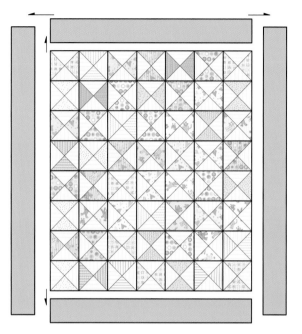

6. Layer the quilt top with batting and backing; baste. Quilt as desired. Sew the 1½"-wide green strips together end to end to make one long strip. Use this strip to bind your quilt. (See "Finishing" on page 76.)

Break Your Bread, Don't Cut It

Dress up your table with this pretty table runner. Depending on the number of charm squares you have, you can make it as long or as short as you like. We love the look of the half-hexagon shape, and there are no inset seams or difficult bindings in this project.

Quilt size: 8¾" x 16"

Materials

Yardages are based on 42"-wide fabric.

15 charm squares, 5" x 5", in two main colors (red and brown)
⅓ yard of fabric for backing
10" x 17" piece of batting
Template plastic★
★*A half-hexagon acrylic template is also available. Check your local quilt shop or Country Threads.*

Still Charming

If you don't have a set of precut charm squares, you'll need a 6" x 7" piece *each* of 10 different fabrics in two main colors (red and brown). Cut each fabric into three half hexagons (30 total).

Cutting

From *each* charm square, cut:
2 half hexagons (30 total) using the pattern on page 61 and the template plastic. See "Working with Templates" on page 75. You can stack up to six charm squares and cut all six at once.

Pioneer Spirit

Using charm packs can be a challenge for those of us who like complete control over the fabrics in our quilts. Most of the rows in the table runner alternate red and brown prints, but our charm pack had an uneven number of red and brown prints, so this is not true for all of the rows. If you have an uneven number of fabrics in each color, you too will have fabrics of the same color side by side. That's OK! Our imperfect projects will resemble those of quilters before us who used what was available, not what was perfectly coordinated.

Assembly

1. Place a red and a brown half hexagon right sides together and offset so the fabric edges meet at the ¼" seam allowance; stitch. Add a third half hexagon to the other side of the brown fabric. For most of the units, we alternated the red and the brown fabrics, making about half of the units with two red and one brown fabric and half with two brown and one red fabric.

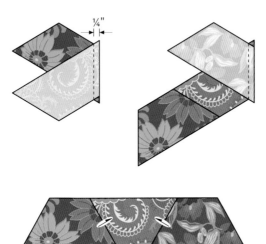

2. Arrange the half hexagons in 10 columns of three each as shown. Sew the columns together. Press the seam allowances in opposite directions from column to column.

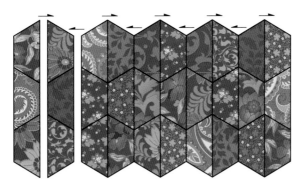

3. Layer the batting, followed by the backing, right side up, and then the quilt, right side down.

4. Stitch along each zigzag edge using a ¼" seam allowance and leaving both ends of the table runner open. With the needle down, pivot at each point and keep stitching. Do not take it out of your machine at each point.

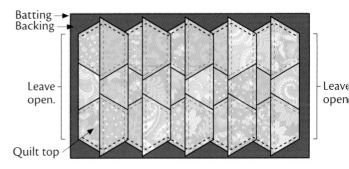

5. Trim the backing and batting around the shape of the runner. Clip up to the seam allowance in the inner points and trim the outer points.

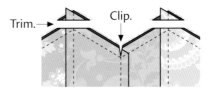

6. Turn the runner right side out. Reach inside with a letter opener or something pointed to push each of the points out.
7. Close each end by hand, turning in ¼" and slip stitching. Press.
8. Machine quilt ¼" from the edges and as desired.

More Is Merrier

If you have a long table, you can extend the runner by choosing a larger charm pack, or supplementing (if necessary) from your fabric collection. Cut 96 half-hexagons and follow the instructions above to join them in 32 columns with three half hexagons per row. Your runner will measure 8¾" x 48½". Use a 10" x 50" piece of batting and 10" x 50" backing.

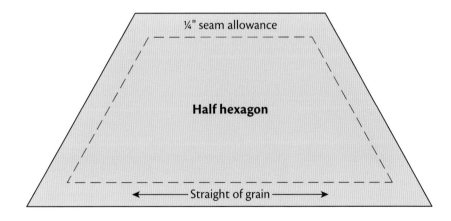

¼" seam allowance

Half hexagon

Straight of grain

Take Compliments Courteously

Yo-yos are usually used as an embellishment, but we thought it would be fun to make an entire project with them. Place this little charmer on a small table, and you'll be sure to receive lots of compliments!

Quilt size: 9¾" x 9¾"

Materials

40 charm squares, 5" x 5"
Quick Yo-Yo Maker from Clover: size large
    OR template plastic

Still Charming

If you don't have a set of charm squares, you'll need a 5" x 20" strip *each* of 10 different prints of varying colors and values. Cut and make four yo-yos from each print

Assembly

The Quick Yo-Yo Maker is great for making quick, easy, and nicely shaped yo-yos, each uniform in diameter. Follow the manufacturer's instructions to make 40 yo-yos; then skip to step 4. If you don't have the yo-yo maker, start at step 1.

1. Make a template using the pattern on page 64, referring to "Working with Templates" on page 75 as needed. From each charm square cut a circle using the template (40 total).

2. Fold under ¼" around the edge of the circle and finger-press. Leaving about a 5" tail, sew a running stitch by hand just inside the edge of the fold.

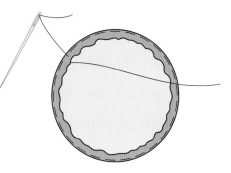

3. Pull the thread to gather the circle into a yo-yo. Tie the thread ends in a knot to secure.

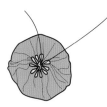

4. Join 40 yo-yos together in the desired configuration. Take four to five tacking stitches to join the yo-yos. We made six rows of six yo-yos each, and then added a yo-yo to each corner.

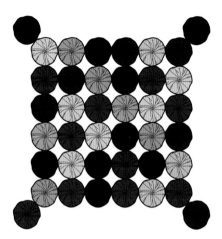

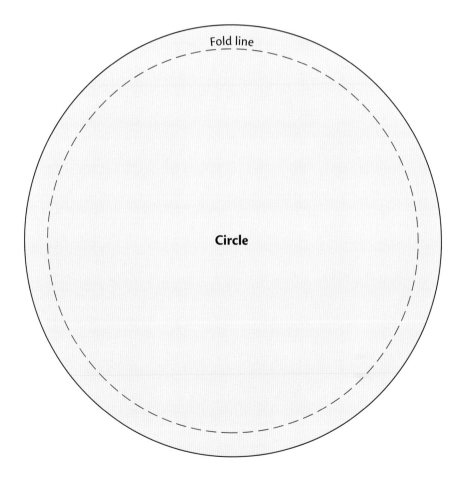

Fold line

Circle

Don't Break Bread into Your Soup

Everyone will use their best table manners in a dining room graced with this elegant quilt.

Quilt size: 27" x 27"
Block size: 4½" x 4½"

Materials

Yardages are based on 42"-wide fabric.

36 charm squares, 5" x 5", in dark to medium values

⅞ yard aged muslin for background★

¼ yard of dark blue fabric for binding

1 yard of fabric for backing

31" x 31" piece of batting

★*If aged muslin is not available, you can substitute regular muslin or an off-white tone-on-tone print.*

Still Charming

If you don't have a set of precut charm squares, you'll need a 5" x 10" piece *each* of at least 18 different prints; half medium value and half dark value. (Using additional fabrics will make your quilt look more like the sample.) When following the cutting list below, cut your prints as indicated for the charm squares, but double the amounts.

Cutting

Measurements include ¼"-wide seam allowances.

Sort charm fabrics into pairs of a medium- and a dark-value fabric (two contrasting fabrics).

From *each* charm square, cut:

4 squares, 2⅜" x 2⅜"; cut each square in half diagonally to make 2 triangles (8 per fabric; 288 total). Keep medium- and dark-value pairs of fabrics together.

From the muslin, cut:

7 strips, 2⅜" x 42"; cut into 108 squares, 2⅜" x 2⅜". Cut each square in half diagonally, to make 2 triangles (216 total).

4 strips, 2" x 42"; cut into 72 squares, 2" x 2"

From the dark blue fabric, cut:

3 strips, 1½" x 42"

Assembly

Work with one medium/dark fabric pair at a time. Each pair will make two identical blocks.

1. Sew a dark fabric triangle and a muslin triangle together as shown. Make three. Repeat with medium fabric triangles and muslin triangles to make three more triangle squares. Make one triangle square with a dark and a medium triangle. Press the seam allowances toward the darker fabrics.

Make 3.   Make 3.   Make 1.

2. Arrange the triangle squares from step 1 with two muslin squares, being careful to position the dark and medium triangles accurately. Sew the units into rows; then sew the rows together. Press. You may find that pressing the seam allowances open makes it easier to match the points. Repeat to make 36 blocks (18 sets of two identical blocks).

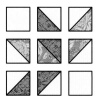

Make 2
identical blocks.

3. Choose two sets of two identical blocks for each four-block unit. Position blocks to form a "circle" and sew together. Press. Make nine four-block units.

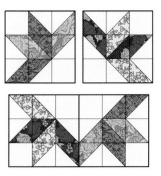

4-block unit.
Make 9.

4. Sew the four-block units together into three rows of three units each. Press rows in opposite directions. Sew the rows together and press.

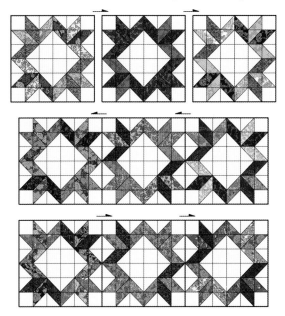

5. Layer the quilt top with batting and backing; baste. Quilt as desired. Sew 1½"-wide dark blue strips together end to end to make one long strip. Use this strip to bind your quilt. (See "Finishing" on page 76.)

Eat Slowly, It Took a Long Time to Prepar

It may take a little longer

to prepare than dinner, but

this elegant little quilt is

worth every minute!

Quilt size: 18" hexagon

Materials

Yardages are based on 42"-wide fabric.

36 charm squares, 5" x 5"
⅛ yard of light brown print for binding
¾ yard of fabric for backing
22" x 25" piece of batting
Template plastic★
★*A half-hexagon acrylic template is also available. Check your local quilt shop or Country Threads.*

Still Charming

If you don't have a set of precut charm squares, you'll need a 5" x 9" piece *each* of 18 different fabrics. (Using additional fabrics will make your quilt look more like the sample.) Cut each fabric into four half hexagons (72 total).

Cutting

Measurements include ¼"-wide seam allowances.

From *each* charm square, cut:
2 half hexagons (72 total) using the pattern on page 61 and template plastic. See "Working with Templates" on page 75. You can stack up to six charm squares and cut all six at once.

From the light brown print, cut:
2 strips, 1½" x 42"

Assembly

This project requires planning, and it's best to lay out all the pieces on your table or work wall before you start sewing. If you look at the photo on page 68 or the diagram on page 70, you'll notice three pieces are joined together with a Y-seam to make an equilateral triangle. The matching half hexagon is used in the equilateral triangle in the adjacent triangle or row. In addition, in every second triangle, the half hexagons are arranged in a reversed (mirror) image of the triangle preceding it. Each row consists of equilateral triangles sewn together with straight seams before the rows are sewn together—but all must match up correctly. (This is *not* a simple Nine Patch quilt!)

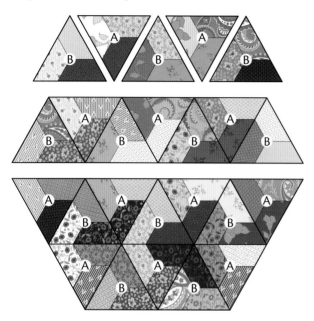

1. You may find it easiest to sew one triangle and put it back in place before sewing the next one. Flip one half hexagon onto another, right sides together, and sew the first seam, stopping ¼" from the inner point. Finger-press the pieces open.

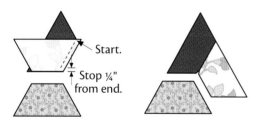

2. Add the third half hexagon and sew the second seam the same way, stopping ¼" from the center.

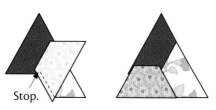

3. Sew the first and the third half hexagons together on the adjoining edge, stopping ¼" from the center. Press seam allowances open. You now have one equilateral triangle.

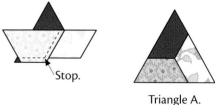

Triangle A.
Equilateral.

4. The triangles adjacent to the first one are a reversed image. Sew in the same manner as triangle A, stitching each seam and stopping ¼" from the center. Continue sewing three half hexagons into equilateral triangles, being careful to sew the matching fabrics in the correct positions.

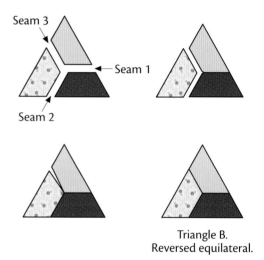

Triangle B.
Reversed equilateral.

5. Make 12 equilateral triangles and 12 reversed equilateral triangles (24 total).
6. Sew the triangles into rows; then sew the rows together and press.
7. Layer the quilt top with batting and backing; baste. Quilt as desired. Sew the 1½"-wide light brown strips together end to end to make one long strip. Use this strip to bind your quilt, pivoting at each corner, and then continuing on. (See "Finishing" on page 76.)

Eat Soup with the Side of Your Spoon

Rules of behavior imply there is only one right way to do things, like how to politely and gracefully eat soup, but quilting is not like that! There are many techniques and block variations open to the quilter. This project can give exciting, different results if you substitute a neutral fabric for one of the charm rectangles in step 1.

Quilt size: 14½" x 32⅝"
Block size: 3⅝" x 3⅝"

Materials

Yardages are based on 42"-wide fabric.

36 charm squares, 5" x 5", for blocks
¼ yard of teal print for binding
⅝ yard of fabric for backing
19" x 37" piece of batting

Still Charming

If you don't have a set of precut charm squares, you'll need a 5" x 10" piece of at least 18 coordinating prints. (Using additional fabrics will make your quilt look more like the sample.) Cut each print into four rectangles, 2½" x 5" (72 total).

Cutting

Measurements include ¼"-wide seam allowances.

From *each* charm square, cut:
2 rectangles, 2½" x 5" (72 total)

From the teal print, cut:
3 strips, 1½" x 42"

Assembly

1. Randomly sew two rectangles together, mixing the fabrics. Press the seam allowances open. Repeat for the remaining rectangles.

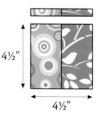

Make 36.

2. Trim the rectangle units to measure 4½" x 4½". Draw a line diagonally from corner to corner. Cut each square along the line to make two triangles (72 total).

4½"

4½"

3. Sew two triangles together, randomly mixing the fabrics. Press in either direction. Make 36 blocks.

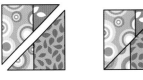

Make 36.

4. For a table runner, arrange blocks in nine rows of four blocks each. Sew the blocks into rows, pressing in opposite directions from row to row. Sew the rows together and press.

5. Layer the quilt top with batting and backing; baste. Quilt as desired Sew 1½"-wide teal strips together end to end to make one long strip. Use this strip to bind your quilt. (See "Finishing" on page 76.)

What If …

I'm sure that while you've worked on a project you've wondered, "What if I changed this?" As I finished this project, we envisioned using a neutral or solid fabric as one of the rectangles. If you'd like to try this variation, in addition to the charm pack, you'll need ¾ yard of a neutral or solid fabric. Also increase the amount of batting and backing fabric.

Cut nine strips of the neutral fabric, 2½" x 42"; then cut the strips into 72 rectangles, 2½" x 5". In step 1, sew each charm rectangle to a neutral rectangle. In step 2, you can either cut all of the squares in the same direction or cut half in one direction and half in the other direction. Whichever way you cut, the resulting triangles can be put together in different ways. You'll end up with 72 blocks, doubling the length of the table runner. For a wall hanging, set the blocks in nine rows with eight blocks per row to make a 29" x 32⅝" quilt.

Squares cut in the same direction

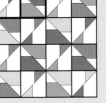

Half of the squares cut right to left; half cut left to right

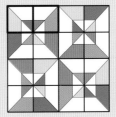

Charm School Techniques

All of the quilts in this book are small and are perfect for learning something new. Maybe you've never worked with templates or tried to machine quilt. With that in mind, we've put together some of the basics you need to know to make the projects.

Working with Charm Squares

Charm-square packets are produced by the fabric manufacturers to help sell their fabric lines. There are luscious feature fabrics, wonderful companion prints, different colorways of the same designs, and everything goes together beautifully. Who can resist? The downside is that a pack with specific fabrics may be available for only a short period of time, so the chance of finding charm packs just like the ones we used is slim. In addition, you're working with a limited number of fabrics and won't be able to control how much of each color or value you have.

When deciding which fabric to use for a specific piece, look at your charm squares in terms of whether the individual squares blend together or are easy to tell apart. We usually think first about different colors, but often this decision has more to do with value—whether the squares are lighter or darker than each other. Difference in value, and whether pieces blur together or contrast, is what creates a quilt design.

Your charm pack probably won't be evenly divided into different values or colors. Ours weren't either! Look at the photos of our quilts, and you'll see some blocks where the individual pieces blend together and others where they're distinct. It's all a matter of "making do with what you have," just as quilters have done for many years.

Compare this version of "Walk—Don't Run" with the photo on page 35.

Cutting

Charm School has one main rule, our 3-Cs Rule: Cut Charms Carefully!

Some of the projects use every bit of each charm square, so there's no room for mis-cuts. We suggest you use a new blade in your rotary cutter and take your time measuring and cutting. If you do ruin a charm square, don't panic! Chances are there's something in your stash you can use as a substitute. It doesn't have to match perfectly, just enough so it blends with the other fabrics. Some charm squares have pinked edges and the 5" measurement goes to the outside edge of the pinking. If you don't need to use all 5", you can trim off the pinked edges—but double-check to be certain before you cut.

Working with Templates

Most of the projects in this book are designed for rotary cutting, but some require templates, the patterns for which appear in the projects. Many acrylic templates are available for purchase at your local quilt shop or Country Threads. You can also make templates from plastic or heavy cardstock. (The insert cards in magazines are a nice weight.) Template plastic is easy to see through, so tracing the shape is quick and easy. If you use cardstock, hold the pattern against a light source, like a window, to see the pattern. Use a permanent marking pen to trace the pattern shape onto the template material. Use paper or craft scissors to cut along the line. Mark the pattern name and grain line on the right side of the template and mark seam intersections to make joining pieces easier. All patterns for piecing include ¼" seam allowances.

If the pattern is not symmetrical, take care that both the fabric and the template are right side up before marking and cutting—otherwise the piece will be the wrong shape. Place the template on the right side of the fabric and with a pencil or removable fabric pen, trace around the edges and mark the seam intersections. Cut along the line. If the lines of the pattern are straight, you can stack up to six fabrics and cut all six at once with a rotary cutter and ruler.

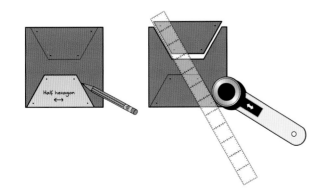

Fusible Appliqué

Always follow the manufacturer's instructions for applying fusible web.

1. Trace or draw your shape on the paper side of fusible web. Cut out the shape, leaving a generous margin all around the outline.

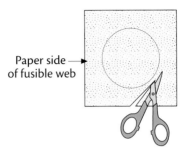

Paper side of fusible web

2. Fuse the shape to the wrong side of your fabric and cut out the shape exactly on the line.

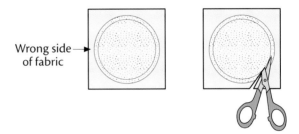

Wrong side of fabric

3. Remove the paper, position the shape right side up on the background and fuse in place.

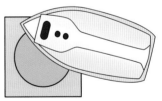

4. If desired, secure the edges with a zigzag or blanket stitch. We like the blanket stitch on our sewing machine, but you can also do this stitch by hand with pearl cotton or embroidery floss.

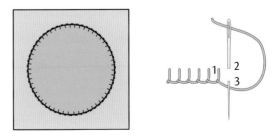

Squaring Up Blocks

When your blocks are complete, take the time to square them up. Use a large square ruler to measure your blocks and make sure they are the desired size plus an extra ¼" on all sides for seam allowances. For example, if you're making blocks that are 4" finished, they should all measure 4½" before you sew them together. Trim the larger blocks to match the size of the smallest one. Be sure to trim all four sides; otherwise your blocks will be lopsided.

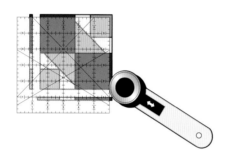

Finishing

You might send your larger quilts to a professional quilter, but these quilts are small enough that it's easy to finish them yourself.

Layering the Quilt

The quilt sandwich consists of backing, batting, and the quilt top. Cut the batting and backing at least 2"–4" larger than the quilt top. We often use low-loft, dense fleece instead of batting for wall hangings and table runners.

1. Spread backing, wrong side up, on a flat, clean surface. Anchor the edges with masking tape. Be careful not to stretch the backing out of shape.
2. Spread the batting over the backing, smoothing out any wrinkles.
3. Place the pressed quilt top on the batting, right side up. Smooth out any wrinkles and make sure the edges of the quilt top are parallel to the edges of the backing.

4. Baste the layers together with pins or basting spray. If you use spray, follow manufacturer's instructions and place layers so there are no wrinkles.

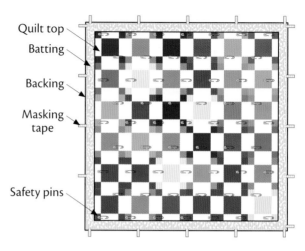

Quilt top
Batting
Backing
Masking tape
Safety pins

If you prefer hand quilting, baste with needle and thread. Start in the center and work diagonally to each corner. Continue basting in a grid of horizontal and vertical lines 6" to 8" apart. Finish basting around the edges.

Quilting

We machine quilted all of the quilts. If you're new to machine quilting, our projects' small size makes them ideal to practice your quilting skills. Your patterns may range from quilting in the ditch and outline quilting to allover free-motion designs. Marking is necessary only if you need to follow a complex pattern. For straight-line quilting, it's absolutely necessary to have a walking foot to feed the quilt layers through the machine without shifting or puckering. You can use masking tape for marking straight lines, but be careful to stitch next to the tape and not over it.

Walking foot

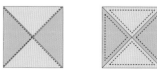

Quilting
in-the-ditch

Outline
quilting

For free-motion quilting, you need a darning foot and the ability to drop the feed dogs on your machine. With free-motion quilting, the machine doesn't move the fabric forward—you do. Instead of turning the fabric under the foot, you guide it in the direction of the design. Use free-motion quilting to outline a pattern or to create stippling or other curved designs.

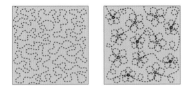

Darning foot

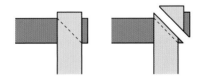

Free-motion quilting

Single-Fold Binding

These are all small quilts and won't get the heavy use a lap or bed quilt receives, so we usually use single-fold straight-grain binding strips. This binding is quick to make and takes less fabric than the more common double-fold bindings.

1. Cut 1½"-wide strips across the width of the fabric. The number of strips to cut is given in each project.

2. Join strips at right angles and stitch across the corner as shown to make one long binding strip. Trim excess fabric and press seam allowances open. Trim the beginning end of the binding strip at a 45° angle, and turn under ¼". Press, being careful not to press out of shape.

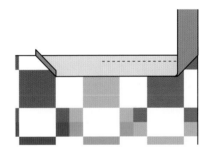

3. Trim the batting and backing even with the quilt top.

4. Starting about midway on one side of the quilt and leaving the first 3" to 4" unsewn, use a ¼"-wide seam allowance to stitch the binding to the quilt, keeping the raw edge of the binding even with the quilt edge. Stop stitching ⅜" from the corner of the quilt and backstitch. Remove the quilt from the machine and clip the thread.

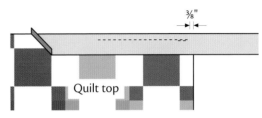

⅜"

Quilt top

5. Turn the quilt so you'll be stitching down the next side. Fold the binding up, away from the quilt.

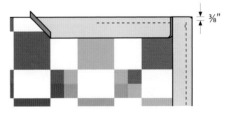

6. Fold the binding back down on itself, parallel with the edge of the quilt. Begin stitching ⅜" from the edge, backstitching to secure, and continue down the next side using a ¼" seam allowance

⅜"

7. Repeat on the remaining sides and corners of the quilt. When you reach the beginning of the binding, overlap the beginning by about 1" and trim any excess binding.

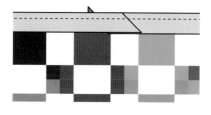

8. Turn the raw edge of the binding under ¼" and fold it to the back of the quilt, covering the line of machine stitching. Blindstitch in place by hand. A miter will form at each corner. Blindstitch the miters and the beginning of the binding strip.

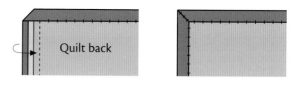

About the Authors

Mary and Connie

Mary Etherington and Connie Tesene have been business partners at Country Threads, Inc. since 1983, shortly after both moved to Garner, Iowa. The business started as a wholesale quilt-pattern company that soon expanded into a retail quilt shop on Mary's small farm in north-central Iowa.

In 1992, That Patchwork Place put Country Threads on the map with the publication of the Quilt Shop Series book about Country Threads Quilt Shop. Customers started walking down the lane with book in hand, and the business began to expand into another building, quilt camps, seasonal events, and a shared desire to keep quilting alive and well.

In 1995, Connie and Mary appeared on the cover of the first issue of *American Patchwork & Quilting* magazine's *Quilt Sampler* after being named one of the first Top Ten quilt shops. In 2008, Connie and Mary were named Entrepreneurs of the Year by *Country Living* magazine.

Today the farm is home to the quilt shop, the wholesale operation, the machine-quilting business, and numerous farm animals, many of whom will greet you when you arrive. Camp is held several times a year in the haymow of the barn, where friends from across the nation gather to sew together for four days.

There's More Online!

If you agree with Country Threads' mission statement (below), you're going to love your visit to the farm—or to the website at www.countrythreads.com. And find more great books on quilting at www.martingale-pub.com.

Connie and Mary have published over 800 individual patterns and more than 20 quilt-pattern books. Even though the business has expanded over the past 27 years, the farm is still home to fancy chickens, geese, goats, dogs, and cats, who greet customers every day. Visitors enjoy the interaction with the cats in the quilt shop and come to know the pets on a personal basis through the *Goat Gazette* newsletter and the free email newsletter.

Our Mission Statement: Country Threads . . . where no goat has ever been denied, no cat has ever been disciplined, and where no dog has ever been discouraged . . . and where quilting is alive and well!

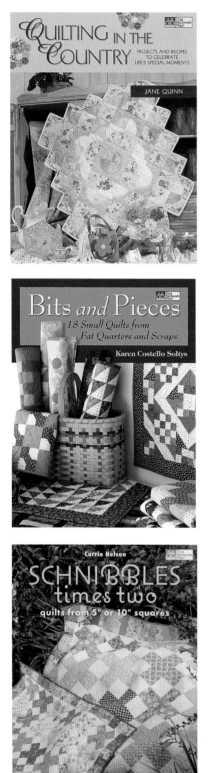

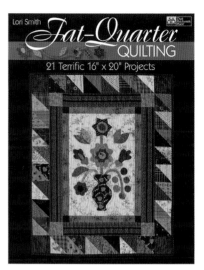